Tap dog Ted

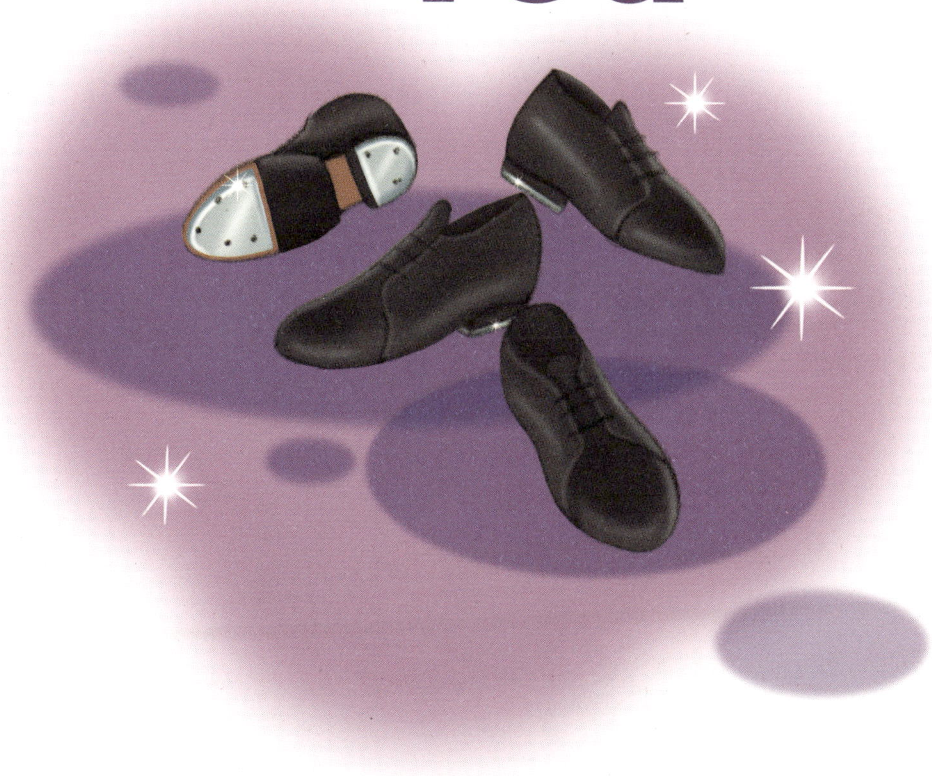

Written by Samantha Montgomerie
Illustrated by Patrizia Manfroi

a Capstone company — publishers for children

Ted loves to tap. Ted tips and taps in his room. He turns and spins to the song. Ted's feet slip and skip and tap.

Ted taps when he is at the swimming pool. Ted taps when he waits in the shop. Ted taps and twists from morning till night.

"I will be a tap dog star!" says Ted.

But Dad says, "Dogs do not tap, Ted. They run for sticks and they dash to get things."

"Wait and see. I **will** be a tap dog star," says Ted.

Parp! Parp! Dad honks the van's horn.
"Come on. We are off to the park!"
says Dad.
"Grab the sticks and get the rings!"
says Spark.
"Off we go!" says Fluff.
They jump into the van.

Dexter skids into Ted's room. Ted is
tip-tapping to the best song ever.
"Come on, Ted. Speed it up and let's go!
We are off to the park," says Dexter.
Ted sighs. He plods to the van with
Dexter.

At the park, the dogs spill out of the van.
Dad sprints and barks as he runs in loops.
Mud flicks up in the air.
Spark wags her tail as she darts to get a stick.
Dexter skips to get a ring.
Splash! Fluff grins as the mud splatters.
"I do not like mud splatters and getting sticks," thinks Ted.

Ted slips off to the trees. He turns and taps. He scuffs his feet as he tip-tip-taps. Ted feels free as he twists and spins in the fresh air. He taps and twists by the trees.

Dad runs to Ted and drops his sticks. "Come and join in. We are splashing in the mud and zooming to get sticks," Dad says.

"I do not like the mud. I do not like getting sticks. I like to tap," says Ted.

"A dog cannot be a tap star, Ted," says Dad. "Darting for rings and dashing to get sticks is fun for dogs. Come and see!"

Fluff runs up. She wags and flicks mud on Ted.
Ted sighs. Tap stars do not like mud.

That night, Mum looks smart in a posh dress. Dad has on his jacket and top hat.
"Tonight is the night of the Bow Wow Hop," Dad tells the pups.
"Will there be a band?" says Fluff.
"Yes. It will be splendid!" says Mum.
Mum spins so that her dress flicks out.

"Will there be twinkling lights?" says Ted.
"Yes!" says Mum.
Ted thinks the Bow Wow Hop will be just right for a tap star.

Ted thinks of a plan.
He gets dressed up. He puts on his best coat with the spots. He puts on his tap boots. He gets out his hat with the glitter on.
Ted looks at himself and grins. He looks like a star!
Ted slips into bed and waits. Mum comes in and kisses his cheek.
"Good night, Ted,"
she says.

Ted waits. He hears footsteps go down the street. Mum and Dad are out!
All is still.
Then he hears the Bow Wow Hop band. He hears the drumming in the night air.
Ted hops out of bed. He creeps by the sitter asleep on a chair. Ted slips out of the room.

Ted puffs and pants as he speeds to the Bow Wow Hop in the moonlight. He can hear the band getting nearer and nearer. Ted cannot wait to get there.

Then, Ted slips off the dark street and into the Bow Wow Hop. The room is spinning in a pool of red and green and pink lights. The lights are like glitter! It is dazzling! It is splendid!

The band's strumming and drumming fill the room.
"It just needs a tap dog star!" thinks Ted.
He feels his feet start to tap.

Ted spins out into the light. His boots tip and tap to the song. Ted grins as he spins. His feet are quick. They tap and flick as he twists and turns.

Ted loves the tap of his feet. He loves the sparkling lights. Ted feels like a star as he clips and clops. He feels free as he twists and taps.

The dogs stop and look at Ted. They start to clap to the song. They wag. They howl. They love Ted!
"Look at his feet!" says Frizz.
"See him spin!" says Bella.
Ted grins as he spins in a pink spotlight. He taps and taps for the crowd.

The band stops. The crowd barks and howls. Ted tips his hat. Flowers rain down on him. Ted bows and bows. He cannot stop grinning!

Mum and Dad rush up to Ted.

"You were fantastic!" says Mum.

"Thanks, Mum," says Ted, blushing.

Dad's tail wags the hardest. He grins from ear to ear.

"You were dazzling, Ted. What a tap star you are!" he says.

"Thanks, Dad," says Ted. Ted's tail wags hard, too.

Next morning, they set off for the park.
Parp! Parp! Mum honks the horn.
"Come on. We are going!" says Mum.
"Grab the rings!" says Spark.
"Get the sticks!" says Dexter.
"Off we go!" says Fluff.
"And pack the tap boots," says Dad.
"I have them right here," grins Ted.